SERVICE CANCELLED

SERVICE CANCELLED

NEIL FULWOOD

All rights reserved. No part of this work covered by the copyright herein may be reproduced or used in any means—graphic, electronic, or mechanical, including copying, recording, taping, or information storage and retrieval systems—without written permission of the publisher.

Printed by imprintdigital
Upton Pyne, Exeter
www.digital.imprint.co.uk

Typesetting and cover design by The Book Typesetters
us@thebooktypesetters.com
07422 598 168
www.thebooktypesetters.com

Published by Shoestring Press
19 Devonshire Avenue, Beeston, Nottingham, NG9 1BS
(0115) 925 1827
www.shoestringpress.co.uk

First published 2021
© Copyright: Neil Fulwood
© Cover painting: Louise Newton
© Author photograph: Dennis Apple

The moral right of the author has been asserted.

ISBN 978-1-912524-80-8

ACKNOWLEDGEMENTS

My thanks to the editors of the following publications where some of these poems, or earlier versions of them, originally appeared: *Central Coast Poetry, Litter, Medusa's Kitchen, New Boots & Pantisocracies, Pendemic, The Platform, The Poetry Bus* and *Rasputin: A Poetry Thread.*

Edward Mackinnon's contribution to 'BWV 34 *O ewiges Feuer, o Ursprung der Liebe*', the final poem in the 'Sacred Cantatas' sequence, is gratefully acknowledged.

My thanks to: Alan Baker, Liz Baugh, Lucy Beckett, Ross Bradshaw, Amy Clarke, Paula Fulwood, Harry Gallagher, Robert Kenchington, Kathy Kieth, John Lucas, Roy Marshall, Judith Rose and Jim Russo; to Louise Newton for providing a stunning cover image; and to family, friends and comrades.

for Harry Paterson

"We have a chance to do something extraordinary. As we head out of this pandemic we can change the world. Create a world of love. A world where we are kind to each other. A world where we are kind no matter what class, race, sexual orientation, what religion or lack of, or what job we have. A world where we don't judge those at the food bank because that may be us if things were just slightly different. Let love and kindness be our roadmap."

– Johnny Corn

CONTENTS

SACRED CANTATAS

BWV 317	3
BWV 108	4
BWV 76	5
BWV 172	6
BWV 132	7
BWV 1	8
BWV 120	9
BWV 5	10
BWV 156	11
BWV 176	12
BWV 39	13
BWV 20	14
BWV 31	15
BWV 14	16
BWV 183	17
BWV 6	18
BWV 82	19
BWV 34	20

THESE EMPTY STREETS

Social Distancing	23
Three Zen Lockdown Poems	24
O Tempora, O Mores	25
How to Survive the Lockdown	26
First of the Day	27
Keg	28
Aqua Vitae	29
Symptom	30
Sentinel	31
Frank O'Hara in the Lockdown	32
Bedtime Story	34
Too Bloody Hot	35
Working from Home	36
Lockdown Sestina	37

Notes	39

Sacred Cantatas

after J.S. Bach

BWV 317
Gott der Vater wohn uns bei

The view is losing the charm it never had.
The house opposite is empty. Closer to home,
litter's gusted round the garden gate,
the lawn's gone native, the hedge is overgrown.

The window's not felt the window-cleaner's touch
for a fortnight now. A lace curtain effect
of half-arsed grubbiness dulls the light.
A neighbour's car leaks oil: the pavement's flecked.

An ice-cream van still makes the rounds, tone-
deaf music blaring. I pause the Bach cantata;
the van's jangling noise subsides. *Gott
der Vater wohn uns bei.* Stay with us, God the Father.

BWV 108
Es ist euch gut, daß ich hingehe

It is for the good that I go away,
or rather remain where I am.

It is for the good that I keep from
the pubs which are shut anyway.

It is for the good that I do not dine
at restaurants which are shut anyway.

That I do not browse
the bookshops which are shut anyway,

catch the latest releases
at cinemas which are shut anyway.

It is for the good, with nowhere
to go, that I remain where I am.

BWV 76
Die Himmel erzählen die Ehre Gottes

The estate as quiet as this: a sure sign
the new normal is anything but.
No youths on unlicensed quad bikes
tear-arsing down the middle of the street,

no cars pulling up near the concrete post,
twists of silver foil changing hands.
No clatter of scarpering heels
through the rat-runs. No sirens wailing closer.

The heavens declare the glory of God.
The police helicopter must be busy elsewhere.

BWV 172
Erschallet, ihr Lieder

The cultural response to lockdown: Italians
taking to balconies with violins,
singing opera from wide-flung windows.

The estate hasn't risen to the moment.
The guy whose white van is sitting silent
could reinvent himself (but doesn't)

as a tool-belt Caruso. The neighbourhood
weed supplier passes up his Oistrakh-
with-an-ASBO chance, gets high instead

on his own supply. Does nobody have a fiddle,
guitar, piano-accordion, penny whistle?
Ring out, songs! A boom box responds. Dismal.

BWV 132
Bereitet die Wege, bereitet die Bahn

A car engine's low growl draws me to the window -
a movie screen finished with ads and trailers,
the main feature about to start. Three doors down,
the guy with the mid-life-crisis Alfa Romeo Giulia

lifts several shopping bags from the boot
with the furtive stumbling haste of a prelate
settling up for his disreputable magazine
in a newsagents several postcode areas away.

Panic buyer. Hoarder. Shelves denuded in his wake.
Prepare the ways, prepare the road, prepare
his uninterrupted final dash from car to front door,
wallet unburdened, unneeded goods to spare.

BWV 1
Wie schön leuchtet der Morgenstern

How beautifully shines the morning star,
how subtly the light of dawn insinuates itself
between the curtains. How flawless the sky
when those curtains are opened, the hangover
blinked away. How welcoming the world

even though the world is boundaried
by the lasso-throw of a postcode area. How
clear the light, how fine-tuned the colours.
How different from the weeks before the crisis
when the skies were grey and hard, the wind

raw and unforgiving, the rain constant.

BWV 120
Gott, man lobet dich in der Stille

(for Amy Clarke)

Confined to quarters is no prison, but still
that bit about the "little tent of blue"
went clomping through my mind the nth day
stood at the window. So I asked you
to send me pictures of a different view.

And you responded in fine style:
the empty acres of Bridgford Park;
a dead calm stretch of the Grantham Canal,
skyline inverted on its glass-still surface;
a weeping willow curating a space

where God might be praised in the stillness.

BWV 5
Wo soll ich fliehen hin

    (for Lucy Beckett)

And where shall I find refuge in the stretches
of these unexpected hours, when nothing moves
on the estate, when curtain-twitching rewards
not with some low-rent *Rear Window* remake
but a freeze-frame of parked vehicles?

Where else but the rabbit-hole of the internet?

Break out the gifs and emojis! Here's clickbait,
memes, quizzes. Here's hours gone by,
mind clouded with the ammonia-soaked rag
of conspiracy theorist piffle. Here's a cat video.
A monkey video. Baby pandas on a slide.

Here's a news update to bring things back to earth.

BWV 156
Ich steh mit einem Fuß im Grabe

I am standing with one foot in the grave, according
to the media, when I'd much prefer the pose
of a stricken Victorian poet reclining on a *chaise longue*,

velvet smoking jacket and a thimble of a glass
brimming with some dull opiate, everything
just terrible, the evening's erotic promises cancelled.

I am standing with one foot in the grave: radio,
TV, the internet insist on it. Texts from government
and NHS reinforce the message. I am a hair's breadth

from being a footnote to a statistic in a news bulletin.
I am a marked man, doomed, blogging on borrowed time.
My cough is receding. My temperature's normal. I feel fine.

BWV 176
Es ist ein trotzig und verzagt Ding

Compress the human soul into a logic box,
make the first choice something daring or shy.
Everything down the line proceeds from this.

Fast forward: no delivery slots for online
shopping, self-isolation locked in place
for three more days. A cupboard audit, then:

a checking of tinned goods' expiry dates.
Two meals instead of three a day: you'll make it.
You'll learn to love that overlooked Pot Noodle.

They'd laugh at you, who made the other choice:
hermits, trappers, mountain men. The kings
of social distancing before it even existed.

BWV 39
Brich dem Hungrigen dein Brot

(for Julie Harrison)

Early, before the bin lorry rumbled
through the empty streets, before

the postman trudged the mossy driveways
with his few slivers of mail, you came to us

bringing bread, freshly baked, smelling better
than any perfume or summer meadow.

And it wasn't only that you gave bread to us,
hungry as we were. It was that you were here

before the bin lorry or the postman,
on an errand we'd not asked of you,

just that you'd woken early and thought of us.

BWV 20
O Ewigkeit, du Donnerwort

    (for Robert Kenchington)

Do the maths: however many hours
times however many days, the view from this
window eternally the same. Time's
not exactly in short supply. A grand project's

what's called for. Me, I'm working my way
through the Bach cantatas. Who on the estate
is similarly engaged? Who's undertaking
the final and definitive curation

of Irish rebel songs? Who's downloaded
every version of 'Body and Soul' and circled
back to Lady Day's? Eternity, O thunderous word,
a fortnight and you've made us connoisseurs.

BWV 31
Der Himmel lacht! Die Erde jubilieret

Heaven laughs! The earth exults. The sky
above the parks and woods and boating lakes
is the blue of postcards and calendars.
Which is all well and good for those for live

within walking distance of parks and woods
and lakes. The rest of us, our once-a-day
period of exercise beginning by order
at our own front door, are gifted a different glory:

a radiance that expands across the estate,
the chippy, the vape shop, the Premier store
bathed in its light. The real-time bus stop signs
blink out their service cancelled message.

BWV 14
Wär Gott nicht mit uns diese Zeit

If God were not with us at this time
would solace be found in this mobile phone app

that totals the number of steps we have taken
around the estate? Would we find our calm

in this broken-concrete pilgrimage; our
hearts' fulfillment? Would we recognise

in these deserted streets, these nervous windows,
in the rammel fly-tipped near the bingo hall

the unimaginable mystery of God's design?

BWV 183
Sie werden euch in den Bann tun

A fortnight of it, climbing the walls.
Armed with an excuse for driving
(as if we would meet blockades,
tanks, men with guns) we set out.

The estate was dead (bad choice
of word); those few out walking
had heads down, eyes turned away:
the etiquette of the prison yard.

We drove; encountered no roadblocks,
saw instead those places forced to close:
the pubs, the hair salons, the coffee shops,
the synagogues they have put you out of.

BWV 6
Bleib bei uns, denn es will Abend werden

A pocketful of mercy, picked by a thief.
Two larks throwing their shadows
across the valley. You never believe
that the worst of the daily news

(dispatches from the deep end
of the doldrums) will affect you
or anyone you know. Then a friend
you messaged for a chat texts you

back and the rug's yanked from beneath
the whole "stay safe" construct.
Their loss. Life taken arbitrarily. Utter grief.
Evening is closing in. Abide with us.

BWV 82
Ich habe genug

   (for Paula)

I am lucky   luckier than many   I have enough
I have warmth and food   I have enough
I am not alone in my own house   I have enough

I have friends and the means of contact   I have enough
A view that's comfortably dull   I have enough
The music of Bach and therefore solace   I have enough

I have books in abundance   I have enough
All the little jobs I now have the time for   I have enough
I have no excuse not to be active   I have enough

I am lucky   luckier than many   I have enough

BWV 34
O ewiges Feuer, o Ursprung der Liebe

(for the keyworkers)

To the nurses, the checkout staff, the delivery drivers:
those our leaders snubbed as unskilled; those
who earn a pittance. They have allowed the rest of us
to withdraw, shut ourselves away, close

the door on social contact, and just maybe flatten
the curve. And those, too, who have made
themselves available, online or over the phone,
to counsel, advise or simply listen.

To the keepers of the eternal fire, the source of love:
these words of thanks when words don't seem enough.

These Empty Streets

SOCIAL DISTANCING

Stay two metres apart. That's six feet
or seventy-two inches. To help visualise
the appropriate distance, pick one of the following
examples. Stay a car length apart

or two car lengths if your car is a Smart Car
or several dozen lengths if it's a toy car.
Stay a small convoy of shopping trolleys apart.
Stay a ping-pong table apart. Take the length

of Evel Knievel's Caesar Palace jump
and divide it by twenty-three
because there's no need to stay that far apart
and we all know how Caesar's Palace turned out.

Stay apart the reach of an average forklift truck
but don't try to emulate it
in terms of weight handling. Stay apart
a decent sized Kenneth Koch poem

printed out in 12-point on A4. Don't go
running after them when the wind
gusts the sheets huffily about
or you might pass closer than two metres.

THREE ZEN LOCKDOWN POEMS

(for Marie Cooper)

1.

Be calm. You no longer have to seek out
the spaces between things. It was not your hand
on the mechanism that widened the vice,
that lifted the drawbridge. It was not your doing,

this silence, this emptying away of activity.

2.

Be calm. The spaces between things
are pockets of thought, periods of silence.
They can be occupied or observed
at a distance. They can be signpost

or sanctuary. They are not absences.

3.

Be calm. The silence need not threaten.
There is opportunity here. Solitude
can be utilised. Enlightenment exists
in the spaces between things,

in the slowing of thought almost to stillness.

O TEMPORA, O MORES

A short stroll, a mere perambulation.
A zone delineated by a radius
extending a half-mile from the house,
if that. We set out, anticipating moderation

from our fellow walkers; expecting
sensible behaviour, the two-metre rule in mind.
But no: they brush past, hover right behind,
jog or cycle too close. We're home now, disinfecting.

HOW TO SURVIVE THE LOCKDOWN

Don't waste your time on those online articles
telling you how to survive the lockdown:
you're an adult, you know to get out of bed
at a certain time, get dressed, tick the box
marked 'rudimentary personal hygiene';
you know the importance of routine,
exercise, discipline. You're an adult, you are capable
of spending a few weeks in your own company,
settling down to some reading, finally listening
to those three hour plus opera recordings
that look good lined up in your CD cabinet.
And those little jobs around the house,
the pruning, cutting and hacking that the garden's
been crying out for - won't it all get done
a little more easily, a little more pleasantly
with Wagner ringing in your ears?

Here's how to survive the lockdown:
ignore all the life-coach nonsense. You're an adult
and it's not as if you can't get through the day
without that keg of Adnams Ghost Ship calling you
like the Devil calling a bluesman
down to the crossroads; it's not as if
you'll tackle the hedge with a bottle of Jim Beam
in one hand and a petrol-driven trimmer
in the other, bellowing a declarative
of the *come and get some if you think
you're hard enough* variety; and it's not as if
you'll find yourself at 3AM in your kitchen,
empty bottles in an honour guard around you,
t-shirt on backwards and a sock on your cock,
watching *Mega Shark vs Giant Octopus* on the iPad,

is it? Of course not. You're an adult. You've got this.

FIRST OF THE DAY

Ad men would reach for images
of cool mountain streams,
chips of ice catching the sunlight
as a skier shoots past.

Rapids, waterfalls, the kind of lagoons
conducive to soft focus
and skinny-dipping. There'd be music
of a sub-Sibelius vintage

and a gravelly voice phrasing homilies
about the clean crisp taste.
None of which are required: merely
a bottle opener, a glass

and the zen-like application of patience
as the beer settles. The long slow
moment of anticipation. The long slow
movement as the glass is raised.

Communion of hops.
John Mills got it right in *Ice Cold
in Alex*. Everything else
is just a sales pitch.

KEG

First vent the keg. Done over bathtub or sink,
a mild hiss of air escaping. Done anywhere
else, a geyser of beer (here's IPA in your eye!)

Next, extract the tap from the base of the keg:
the plastic may snap or your fingernail break
but what's a little discomfort when there's a pint

at the end of it? Hold your glass at an angle;
give the tap a quarter turn. The first glass
will wash with froth. Let it settle. Top it up.

Repeat till pint at line. Drink deeply. Enjoy
your keg, responsibly or otherwise. Dispose
of it other than in someone's swimming pool.

Do not be swayed by your inner frat boy.

AQUA VITAE

Only the tiniest dash of water
and only then if it's a heady, peaty malt.

Warm the glass, cup your hands
around it. Be reverent.

Inhale. Don't be shy. Get your nose
right in the glass; breathe deeply.

What notes are you getting? Heather,
sea air, fruit, hints of caramel?

Or is the smoky insistence of peat
ravaging your nostrils? Raise

your glass, make the toast: *sláinte
mhath*. Take a sip. Feel the burn.

SYMPTOM

Drunk and in charge
of an iPad: the only symptom
you exhibited during the quarantine.

The unfunny tweets,
the maudlin Facebook posts,
the middle-aged embarrassment
you made of yourself on TikTok.

The things you ordered online.

The delivery vans growling to a stop,
the rat-a-tat-tat door knocks,
the parcels left on the welcome mat

and you raising a puzzled hand
to another retreating driver,
wondering
what the hell you bought this time.

SENTINEL

    (for Donna and Alisa)

An hour after I stood at the front door
flinging the length of the driveway
the last scraps of my chicken dinner,
watching them lock on target
like furry missiles,

next door's cats
are still in my front yard, silent and sinister
as tracking stations, attuned to motion,
activity, my shadow at the window,
the chance of the front door opening again.

FRANK O'HARA IN THE LOCKDOWN

Those most conversational of his poems,
the I-do-this-I-do-that ones -
how would they have worked in lockdown?
There'd be the walks, sure,
and the observations of human life
(palimpsests rather than screeds, but hey ho)
and meditations on the deceleration
of the pace of life. But of the trip to the deli
and the sybaritic consumption
of something almost sinful on rye - how
would the absence of that impact
on the poem? Where
would it leave the poem?
Would the poor confused thing
even recognise itself as a poem?
It might at best be able to grab
a coffee in a polystyrene container
from a still-open café serving hot drinks only
from behind a table wedged into the doorway.
But the opportunity
to sit by the window and philosophically
pour cream into that coffee - and add
sugar by degrees as if the act itself
were sacrament - well, try replicating that
on a street corner with a polystyrene container
while trying to stand two metres distant
from the yahoos jogging past
or wobbling all over the place on pushbikes.
And try replicating the stunned awareness
at a newspaper headline
when the only thing outside the paper shop

is a sign saying only two customers
allowed in at any one time. And slang-
infused conversations with a shoe-shine boy?
Forget about it. May as well just
noodle on your iPhone while you walk
the same route through the estate,
past the locked-up play park, back the way
the number 15 bus goes, and home.

BEDTIME STORY

Down the rabbit hole, folks,
through the looking glass,
the Mad Hatter's in control
and he hates the underclass.

There's a tea party here, folks,
for Earl Grey's posh pals only.
The underclass they have no beer
now the pubs are closed. It's lonely

in not-so-wonderful wonderland, folks,
and the lack of fun never stops.
The Blue King's methods are underhand
and the playing cards are cops.

Off with the poet's head, folks,
decapitate the dissenter.
"Hail the Blue King," declares
the BBC presenter.

The rabbit hole emerges, folks,
in the square of the polling booth.
The Cheshire Cat grins with unhealthy urges
but the fox has a sharper tooth;

a sharper claw as well, folks,
as the Blue King will come to know.
At the fox's command, unleash all hell;
unleash more at the word of the crow.

TOO BLOODY HOT

Too bloody hot, this drowsy Wednesday
in May,
week whatever of the lockdown
and far too easy to play
hooky when you're working from home.
Just keep the work phone

on your person when you set out
for that walk, intending
to amble down to the park. The unrelenting
sun puts paid to that.
Sluggish, sweating,
having left the house without

shades, hat or bottle of mineral water,
you call it less than half way
there, about face, cross the road (more to
seek shade than socially
distance) and walk back. Slowly.
You tell yourself you'll go out again later

in the cool of the evening, seven
or maybe eight o'clock. But
you know that's baloney. You've got
a cold one in the fridge. More than
one, in fact. By the time it's
cool enough to head out again

you'll be on your second or third,
the chilled surface
of the bottle pressed
against your forehead,
a lace
of froth patterning the glass.

WORKING FROM HOME
(for Paula)

The office as ghost town,
a scrap of paper near the shredder
standing in for a tumbleweed.

The photocopier looms silent
and implacable as a monolith.
Filing cabinets invite comparison

to old films about espionage
where files reside in dusty rooms.
The office jumbles genres

but perhaps more than anything
captures the atmosphere
of an art-house film, endless

static shots of ordinary things,
the camera holding on them
so long that they slip the holdings

of their context, become abstract.

LOCKDOWN SESTINA

Normality has come to
an impasse. The world shrinks
to a small web of streets,
everyday life to these
four walls. Everything
beyond the window is empty.

Empty streets, cars empty
of passengers. Buses, too:
with everything
closed down, travel shrinks
to supermarket trips. Those
bustling city streets

are silent now. Streets
grim with shutters, empty
windows. How many of these
places will reopen, and to
what custom? Income shrinks
across the board; everything

looks bleak. Everything
seems surreal, streets
not even gusted with the shrink-
wrappings of litter, empty
premises hung with signs to
the effect of "these

are temporary measures". These
measures might not be. Everything
depends on those to
whom the man in the street
is expendable: the empty-
hearted politicians who shrink

from responsibility, who shrink
into the bluster of these
post-truth times. Empty
of empathy, they forget: everything
is microcosm. These are streets
the privileged don't belong to.

Everything shrinks
to these
empty streets.

NOTES

BWV 120 Gott, man lobet dich in der Stille
The phrase "little tent of blue" references Oscar Wilde's 'The Ballad of Reading Gaol'.

BWV 6 Bleib bei uns, denn es will Abend werden
The phrase "pocketful of mercy" references the Led Zeppelin song 'In the Evening' (*In Through the Out Door*, Swan Song, 1979). "Two larks throwing their shadows / across the valley" references 'Im Abendrot' by Joseph von Eichendorff, set by Richard Strauss as one of his *Vier letzte Lieder*.

Too Bloody Hot
The phrase "a cold one in the fridge" references the song of the same title by Paul Heaton (*Acid Country*, Proper Records, 2010).

Bedtime Story
The touchstone here is, of course, Lewis Carroll. Fox and Crow have wandered in from the works of Ted Hughes.